CW01651583

BIRDS

STICKER FUN

Miles Kelly

First published in 2003 by Miles Kelly Publishing Ltd
Harding's Barn, Bardfield End Green, Thaxted, Essex, CM6 3PX, UK

This edition printed in 2012

2 4 6 8 10 9 7 5 3 1

Publishing Director Belinda Gallagher
Creative Director Jo Cowan
Project Manager Nicola Sail
Edition Editor Amanda Askew
Cover Designer Kayleigh Allen
Designer Maya Currell
Reprographics Stephan Davis
Production Manager Elizabeth Collins

British Library Cataloguing-in-Publication Data
A catalogue record for this book is available from the British Library

ISBN 978-1-84810-625-3

Printed in China

COVER Lindsey Eltinge/Shutterstock, BG Inga Nielsen/Shutterstock;
BACK COVER tl Volodymyr Krasyuk/Shutterstock; 2bl xpixel/Shutterstock; 3b Fotolia
All other images are from the MKP archives

www.mileskelly.net
info@mileskelly.net

www.factsforprojects.com

INTRODUCTION

Almost anywhere in the world, you will see birds. A bird is warm-blooded, has two legs, a pair of wings and a body covered with feathers.

There are almost 9000 kinds of bird. They live everywhere from the cold ice of Antarctica to the hot deserts of Africa. They range in size from the huge ostrich – taller than a human adult – to the tiny bee hummingbird that is not much bigger than a real bee!

With this great sticker book you can learn about all different kinds of birds and impress your friends with amazing facts!

Mini stickers!

Does the albatross live high in the mountains or near to the sea? What about the huge ostrich – is it found in cold icy places or open grassland? Use your mini stickers to see where some of the world's birds are found!

Coastal/Ocean – most birds that live here feed on fish and many build their nests on clifftops

River/Lake – waterbirds mostly feed off the water surface, but some dive for fish and other food

Mountain – birds that live here fly high on mountain winds and feed mainly on smaller animals

Forest – provides birds with plenty of food and places for nesting

Polar – many birds have white feathers to blend with their snowy surroundings

Rainforest – over 4000 kinds of birds are found in the warm and wet rainforests

Desert/Grassland – many birds which live here have sandy-brown feathers to blend with their surroundings and hide from their enemies

Coastal/Ocean

▲ Wilson's storm petrel

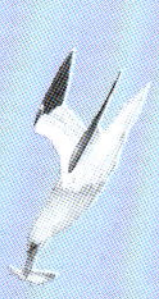

▲ Northern gannet

▲ Blue-footed booby

▲ Avocet

▲ Wrybill

▲ Wandering albatross

▲ Atlantic puffin

River/Lake

▲ Flamingo

▲ Mallard

▲ Whistling swan

▲ Malachite kingfisher

▲ Canada goose

Mountain

▲ Golden eagle

▲ Andean condor

Forest

▲ Tawny frogmouth

▲ Barn owl

Polar

▲ Snowy owl

▲ Arctic tern

▲ Emperor penguin

Rainforest

▲ Male peacock

▲ Scarlet macaw

▲ Sword-billed hummingbird

▲ Sunbittern

▲ Toco toucan

▲ Hoopoe

▲ Superb fairy wren

Desert/Grassland

▲ Ostrich

▲ Egyptian vulture

▲ Elf owl

▲ Sandgrouse

▲ Greater roadrunner

▲ Great bustard

Birds of the world

▼ Wandering albatross
Biggest seabird with a wingspan of 3 metres

▶ Scarlet macaw
Flies through the forest at up to 56 kilometres an hour

▼ Male peacock
Has a long train of feathers that it uses to attract a female

◀ Malachite kingfisher
Makes its nest in a riverbank tunnel that is up to 60 centimetres l

▶ Mallard
Male has a low-pitched quack and a sharp whistle

▼ Whistling swan
Thought to be the bird with the most feathers – over 25,000

◀ Egyptian vulture
Cracks open eggs by throwing stones at them

▶ Northern gannet
May dive after prey from up to 45 metres above the water

KEY: Coastal/Ocean, River/Lake, Mountain, Forest, Polar, Rainforest, Desert/Grassland

◀ Arctic tern
Travels further than any other bird from the Arctic to the Antarctic

▼ Sunbittern
Name comes from the red-orange markings on its wings

▼ Blue-footed booby
Attracts mate by dancing and drawing attention to its colourful feet

▲ Avocet
Sweeps bill through shallow water to find food

▼ Andean condor
Biggest type of vulture with the largest wing area of any bird

▶ Tawny frogmouth
Can disguise itself to look like a branch or tree stump

▼ Greater roadrunner
Swift running bird that reaches speeds of up to 30 kilometres an hour

◀ Superb fairy wren
Male may give the female a yellow flower petal during mating display

Penguins huddle together for warmth while they look after their eggs. They take it in turns to stand on the outside and take the full force of the cold winds!

The biggest bird

The world's largest bird is the ostrich. This long-legged bird stands up to 2.8 metres tall and weighs up to 160 kilograms – twice as much as an average adult human. Although too heavy to fly, it can run at up to 70 kilometres an hour for as long as 30 minutes!

The female ostrich lays the biggest of all birds' eggs. At up to 20 centimetres long, one egg would make about 12 omelettes!

Birds of the world

▲ Whistling swan

▲ Egyptian vulture

▲ Scarlet macaw

▲ Northern gannet

▲ Malachite kingfisher

▲ Male peacock

▲ Mallard

▲ Wandering albatross

◀ Whistling swan

▶ Egyptian vulture

◀ Scarlet macaw

◀ Northern gannet

▼ Male peacock

◀ Malachite kingfisher

▼ Wandering albatross

▲ Mallard

Birds of the world

▲ Superb fairy wren

▲ Greater roadrunner

▲ Andean condor

▲ Tawny frogmouth

▲ Blue-footed booby

▲ Sunbittern

▲ Arctic tern

▲ Avocet

▶ Superb fairy wren

▼ Greater roadrunner

◀ Andean condor

▼ Tawny frogmouth

▲ Blue-footed booby

▶ Sunbittern

▶ Arctic tern

▲ Avocet

▼ Sword-billed hummingbird

▶ Flamingo

◀ Wilson's storm petrel

◀ Golden eagle

▶ Snowy owl

▲ Wrybill

▼ Great bustard

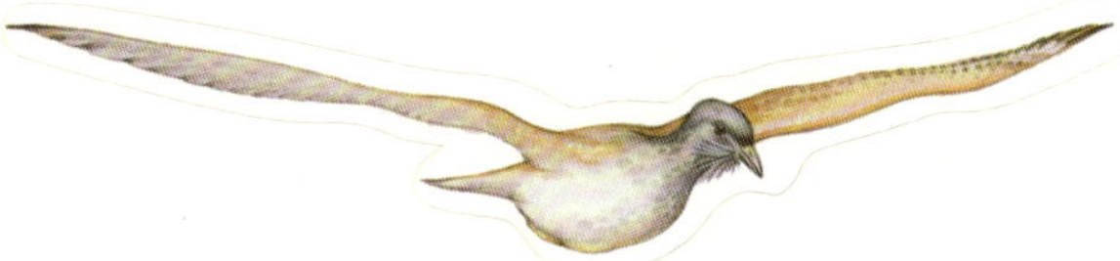

▶ Barn owl

▲ Sword-billed hummingbird

▲ Flamingo

▲ Wilson's storm petrel

▲ Golden eagle

▲ Snowy owl

▲ Wrybill

▲ Barn owl

▲ Great bustard

Birds of the world

▼ Ostrich

▶ Emperor penguin

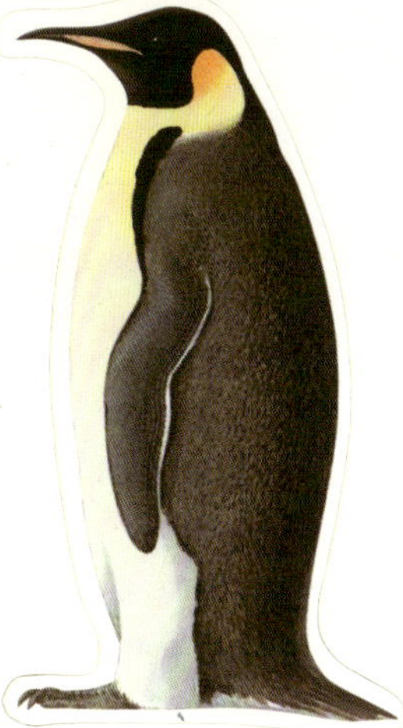

▼ Hoopoe

▼ Toco toucan

▲ Canada goose

▼ Sandgrouse

▼ Atlantic puffin

◀ Elf owl

▲ Ostrich

▲ Emperor penguin

▲ Hoopoe

▲ Toco toucan

▲ Canada goose

▲ Sandgrouse

▲ Atlantic puffin

▲ Elf owl

Golden bird

The golden eagle is one of the fiercest of all birds of prey. These are birds which hunt other animals. The eagle has very good eyesight and sees objects from a far greater distance than you can.

The golden eagle usually lays two eggs. The first chick to hatch often kills the younger chick. At first the mother keeps the surviving chick warm while the male finds food, but as the chick grows larger, both parents are kept busy supplying it with food.

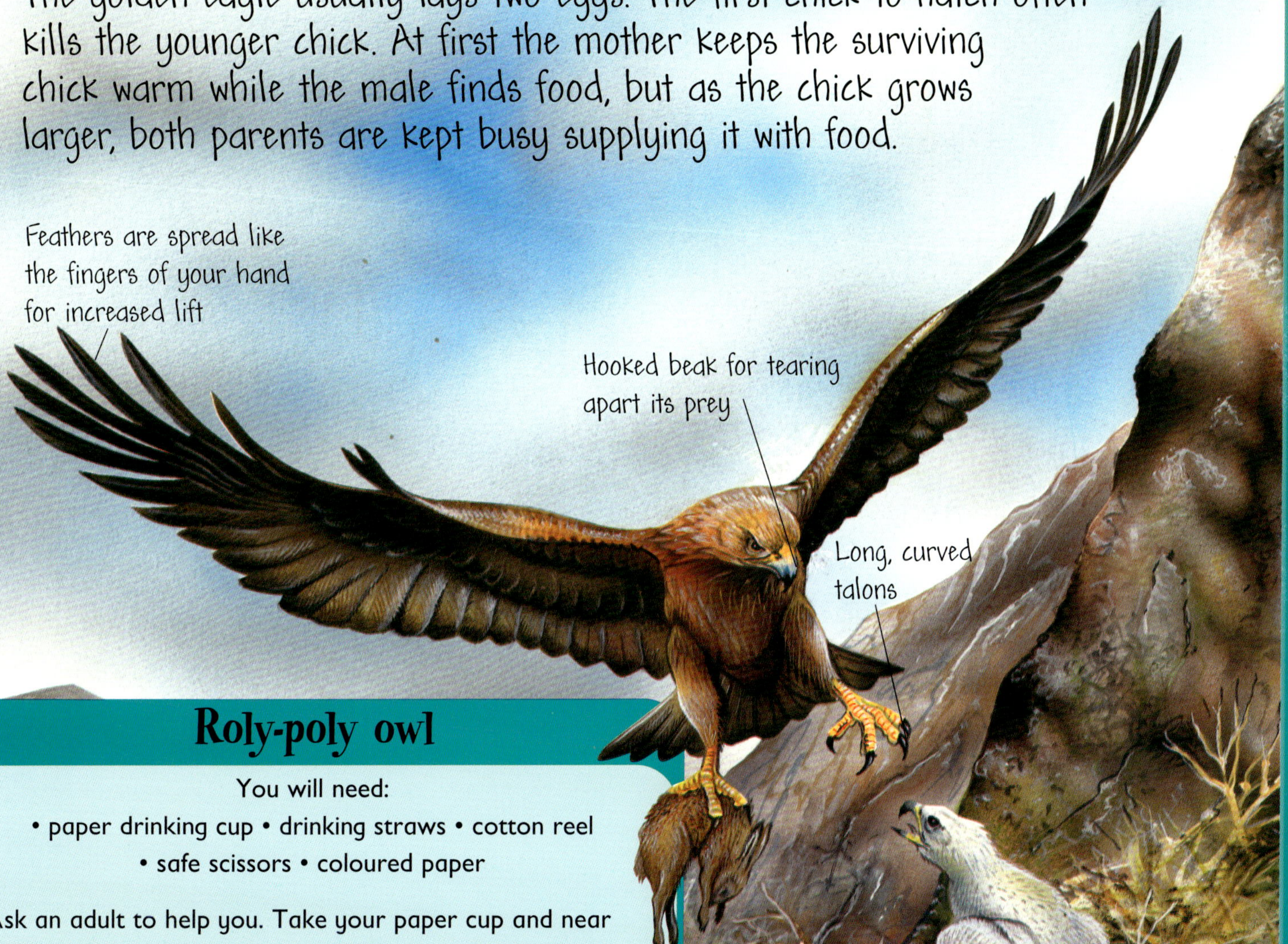

Roly-poly owl

You will need:
• paper drinking cup • drinking straws • cotton reel
• safe scissors • coloured paper

1. Ask an adult to help you. Take your paper cup and near the rim put two holes opposite each other. Push a plastic drinking straw through the hole on one side of the pot, through the centre of the cotton reel and out through the hole on the other side.
2. Turn your paper cup upside down so the cotton reel is at the bottom.
3. Cut out six paper circles (three for each eye) and stick them on the pot. Fold up some coloured paper to make wings and a beak.

Birds of the world

◄ Snowy owl
Long, thick feathers cover its body to keep it warm

▼ Great bustard
Heaviest flying bird weighing about 18 kilograms

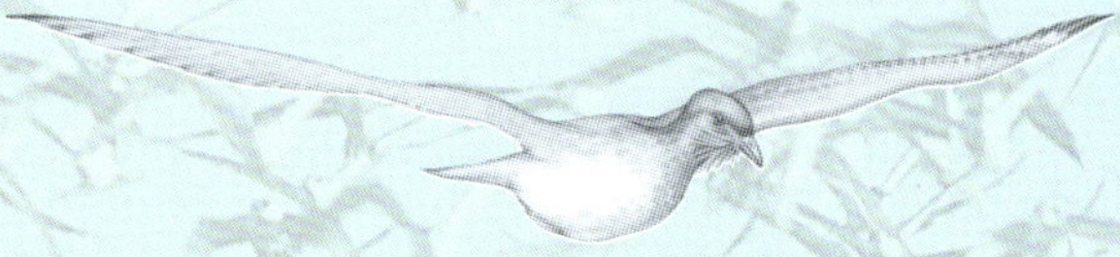

◄ Golden eagle
Has a wingspan of 2.3 metres and is one of the largest eagles

▼ Barn owl
Can hunt in total darkness, locating prey by sound

▲ Wrybill
Only bird with a beak that curves to the right

▲ Wilson's storm petrel
Smallest seabird in the world – only 17 centimetres long

◄ Sword-billed hummingbird
Only bird whose bill is longer than the rest of its body

◄ Flamingo
Uses its beak to filter food from shallow wate

KEY: Coastal/Ocean, River/Lake, Mountain, Forest, Polar, Rainforest, Desert/Grassland

◀ ***Elf owl***

Nests in a hole in a desert cactus, keeping it safe from enemies

▼ ***Sandgrouse***

Has special feathers that act like sponges to hold water, so its young can drink the water from them

▼ ***Atlantic puffin***

Digs a burrow on a clifftop, often taking over a rabbit hole

◀ ***Canada goose***

Spends summer in the Arctic and winter in North America

▶ ***Toco toucan***

Largest of all toucans with a bill up to 19 centimetres long

▼ ***Ostrich***

Largest of all birds but cannot fly

▶ ***Hoopoe***

Has foul-smelling nest which is thought to keep predators away

▲ ***Emperor penguin***

Has wings but cannot fly and spends most of its time in water

The flamingo's legs may look as if they are back to front. In fact, what appears to be the bird's knees are really its ankles!

The biggest and best!

Common swifts may stay in the air for up to four years, sleeping as they fly!

The guillemot lays an egg that is pear-shaped with one end much more pointed than the other. This means that the egg rolls round in a circle if knocked, so it does not fall off the cliff.

Penguins sometimes slide along on their body instead of walking – we call this tobogganing.

Read on to find out about some of the record-breaking birds

- The tiny bee hummingbird is the smallest bird in the world. It measures about 5 centimetres and that includes the length of its bill and tail!

- The fastest swimming bird is the gentoo penguin. It has been known to swim at speeds of up to 27 kilometres an hour!

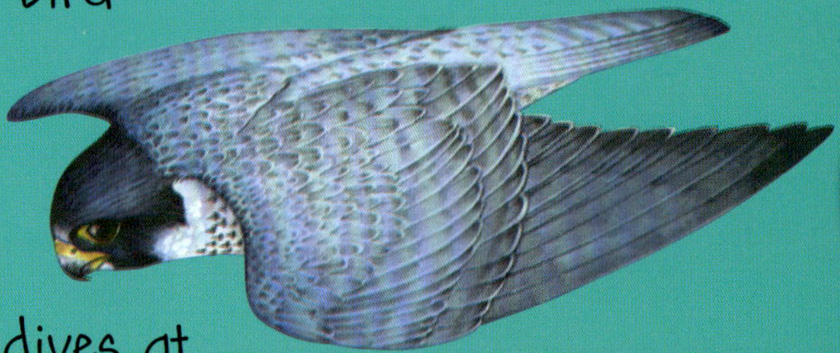

- The fastest flying bird is the peregrine falcon. It hunts other birds and makes spectacular dives at speeds of 200 kilometres an hour.

Q: Which birds spend all the time on their knees?

A: Birds of prey!

Baby birds

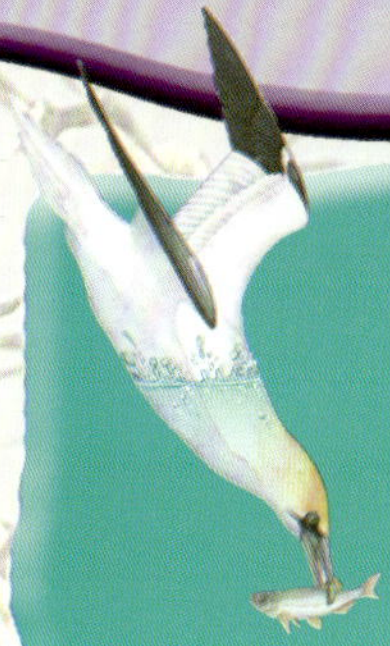

Discover more about how a bird hatches

▶ The baby bird starts to chip away at the egg.

◀ The egg begins to crack.

▶ The egg splits open.

◀ The baby is usually blind and helpless when it first breaks out of the egg.

▶ Most babies are cared for by their parents for several weeks.

Bird facts

The cuckoo can lay her egg in nine seconds. This allows her to pop her egg into a nest while the owner's back is turned!

Water birds called great crested grebes perform a courtship dance together. During the dance they offer each other gifts – beakfuls of water weed!

Vultures have been seen flying as high as a jet plane – at over 11,000 metres!

Q: What do you get if you cross a duck with a firecracker?

A: A firequacker!

Bird facts

When the peregrine falcon swoops on a smaller bird, the force of the impact scatters feathers over a wide area and can knock the victim's head off!

The Australian kookaburra's call sounds like cackling human laughter.

Flamingos are pink because their bodies take on the pink colour of the shrimps they eat. If they don't eat enough shrimps, they turn a dull grey colour.

Test your memory!

How much can you remember from your birds sticker activity book? Find out below!

1. Which bird lays its eggs in the nests of other birds?
2. Which bird runs fastest on the ground?
3. What do great crested grebes give each other during courtship dances?
4. Which rainforest bird is known for its long colourful beak?
5. How fast can a cuckoo lay its egg?
6. Which is the smallest bird in the world?
7. Which bird may stay in the air for as long as four years?
8. Which is the fastest swimming bird?
9. Which is the biggest seabird in the world?
10. How does the Egyptian vulture crack open eggs?

Q: Which bird is always out of breath?
A: A puffin!

Bird facts

11. How does the blue-footed booby attract a mate?
12. Which is the world's tallest bird?
13. Approximately, how many kinds of bird are there?
14. How many eggs does the golden eagle usually lay?
15. Which is the heaviest flying bird?
16. Which is the only bird with a beak that curves to the right?
17. Which rainforest bird has a foul-smelling nest?
18. Which is the only bird with a bill that is longer than its body?
19. Which is the world's fastest flying bird?
20. Which bird's call sounds like cackling human laughter?

Answers:

1. The cuckoo **2.** The ostrich **3.** Water weed **4.** Toco toucan **5.** Nine seconds **6.** Bee hummingbird **7.** The swift **8.** The gentoo penguin **9.** The wandering albatross **10.** By throwing stones at them **11.** By dancing and drawing attention to its feet **12.** The ostrich **13.** Almost 9000 **14.** Two **15.** Great bustard **16.** The wrybill **17.** The hoopoe **18.** The sword-billed hummingbird **19.** The peregrine falcon **20.** The kookaburra

Hummingbirds can fly in all directions – forward, backward, up, down and sideways. They can even hover in one spot.

Flamingos can wade and feed in very salty, shallow lakes where the water is hotter than in our bathtubs.

The northern gannet's head is protected with sacs of air. These absorb most of the shock when it plunges headfirst into the sea, from heights of up to 30 metres.

Q: What do you call a woodpecker with no beak?
A: A headbanger!